WHITE WATER

By S.L. Hamilton

Published by ABDO Publishing Company, 8000 West 78th Street, Suite 310, Edina, MN 55439. Copyright ©2010 by Abdo Consulting Group, Inc. International copyrights reserved in all countries. No part of this book may be reproduced in any form without written permission from the publisher. A&D Xtreme™ is a trademark and logo of ABDO Publishing Company.

Printed in the United States of America, North Mankato, Minnesota.
102009
012010

PRINTED ON RECYCLED PAPER

Editor: John Hamilton
Graphic Design: Sue Hamilton
Cover Design: John Hamilton
Cover Photo: Getty Images
Interior Photos: AP-pg 10; Getty Images-pgs 4, 5, 6, 7, 9, 10, 11, 12, 13, 14, 15, 16, 17, 20, 21, 22, 23, 24, 25, 26, 27, 30, & 31; iStockphoto-pgs 8 & 9; JupiterImages-pgs 2, 3, 18, 19, 28, 29, & 32; National Geographic-pg 1.

Library of Congress Cataloging-in-Publication Data

Hamilton, Sue L., 1959-
  White water / S.L. Hamilton.
     p. cm. -- (Xtreme sports)
  Includes index.
  ISBN 978-1-61613-006-0
  1. White-water canoeing--Juvenile literature. 2. Extreme sports--Juvenile literature. I. Title.
  GV784.3.H36 2010
  796.04'6--dc22
                        2009041268

CONTENTS

XTREME

"If you think you're going to die, you probably will."
~William Neely, kayaker

Xtreme Quote

WHITE WATER

White water is the racing,
violent flows found near
waterfalls and rapids.
With pulse-pounding
speed, kayakers,
canoeists, rafters,
and surfers risk
all to experience
the exciting power
of white water.

WHITE WATER

White water kayaking began thousands of years ago. Modern kayaking is credited to natives of the Arctic. Inuit people put sealskin over wooden frames. Today's kayaks are mostly made of fiberglass or plastic, although there are still wooden models.

KAYAKING

Xtreme Quote

"You'll be OK."
~Called to a kayaker by
someone safe on shore

Difficulty

White water runs are divided into levels of difficulty.
Grade 1–Easy. Fast-moving water.
Grade 2–Novice. Rapids in wide rivers.
Grade 3–Intermediate. Rapids, waves, and tight maneuvers.
Grade 4–Advanced. Intense, powerful rapids and waves.
Grade 5–Expert. Violent rapids and dangerous obstacles.
Grade 6–Extreme. Life threatening and nearly impossible.

Slalom

White water slalom, also known as slalom canoeing, is a popular kayaking sport and Olympic competition. Racers compete by speeding down 300-meter white water tracks. Paddlers must be able to slow down, stop, and turn around obstacles and racing gates.

Gates

Xtreme Definition "Gates" are two poles hanging from wire strung across the water.

Wildwater Racing

Kayakers compete in white water races known as wildwater, or downriver racing. Athletes race downriver, attempting to be the fastest over a track of rapids, rocks, waterfalls, and waves.

Xtreme Fact

Reading a river's obstacles and currents, downriver racers look for the fastest line of travel.

8 Ball

Up to 10 kayakers sprint 200 meters down a white water track. However, they face more than the usual rocks, waves, dips, and rapids. Spoilers, known as 8 ballers, sit waiting in their own kayaks. Dressed in full body armor, the 8 ballers attack the sprinters, doing everything they can to slow down the racers.

"8 Ball... is kayaking's version of NASCAR." ~Teva Mountain Games

Freestyle

Freestyle paddlers take small kayaks called playboats into white water-covered holes. Freestylers then use their bodies to make the boat perform a fun series of twisting, turning moves. Enders, loops, squirts, and spins are judged for difficulty levels and performance success.

WHITE WATER

"High siding" is to lean toward an object that the canoe is about to hit, so your weight is on the high side of the boat.

CANOEING

White water canoeists paddle their open crafts on a rocking, wild, and wet trip down a blasting river. The canoe is often longer and heavier than a kayak. The single-blade paddle is also more challenging to use than a kayak's double-bladed paddle.

WHITE WATER

RAFTING

White water rafts, also called inflatables, are designed to hold several people. Some rafts come with cross tubes, or thwarts. Paddlers use their legs to brace themselves on the thwarts. This makes it possible for rafters to use both hands to paddle.

WHITE WATER

White water surfing is also known as water sliding. It is a dangerous activity requiring superior balance. Sliders begin at the top of a waterfall, running as fast as they can toward the edge. They slide down the falls on the soles of their feet.

SURFING

Xtreme Quote   "Let's do it!"
~Anonymous Surfer

River runners around the world enjoy the fast, foaming excitement of white water.

Colorado River, Arizona

WHITE WATER

Potomac River, Virginia

Itacaré, Bahia, Brazil

Victoria Nile, Uganda, Africa

Elk River, British Columbia, Canada

Strumboding Waterfall, Austria

DANGERS

White water is dangerous. People risk being trapped underwater or knocked out and drowned. Anyone entering white water must wear a helmet and a personal flotation device (PFD).

AND RISKS

Xtreme Quote

"You don't drown by falling into water. You drown by staying there." ~Robert Allen

THE

Arctic
An area near the North Pole.

Ender
A move that brings a kayak into a vertical, up-and-down position. Front enders bring the nose of the kayak into the water. Back enders bring the stern.

Fiberglass
A type of material composed of fine glass fibers embedded in a plastic resin. Fiberglass is strong. It is often used to build canoes and kayaks.

Inuit
People native to the Arctic area.

Loops
A roll where the boater flips the boat lengthwise. It may be performed underwater or in the air.

GLOSSARY

Obstacles
Objects in or under the water, such as rocks or logs.

PFD
A personal flotation device, also known as a life jacket. A life saving device designed to keep a person afloat even if he or she has been knocked out. Different styles are worn by different boaters to allow needed freedom of movement for paddling.

Spin
Making the boat circle a complete 180 degrees, or all the way around .

Squirts
Moves that position a boat from flat to vertical in the water using the hydraulics, or force, of a river.

INDEX